BALTIMORE

A PHOTOGRAPHIC PORTRAIT

Photography by Jake McGuire

Copyright © 2005 by
Twin Lights Publishers, Inc.

All rights reserved. No part of this book may be reproduced in any form without written permission of the copyright owners. All images in this book have been reproduced with the knowledge and prior consent of the artists concerned and no responsibility is accepted by producer, publisher, or printer for any infringement of copyright or otherwise, arising from the contents of this publication. Every effort has been made to ensure that credits accurately comply with information supplied.

First published in the United States of America by:

Twin Lights Publishers, Inc.
8 Hale Street
Rockport, Massachusetts 01966
Telephone: (978) 546-7398
http://www.twinlightspub.com

ISBN-13: 978-1-885435-54-1
ISBN-10: 1-885435-54-1

10 9 8 7 6 5 4 3 2

Frontispiece:
Francis Scott Key Monument with M. W. Prince Hall Grand Lodge of Maryland.

pages 2–3: Maryland Institue of Art

Editorial researched and written by
Francesca Yates and Duncan Yates

Book design by
SYP Design & Production, Inc.
http://www.sypdesign.com

Printed in China

INTRODUCTION

The British mounted their attack against Baltimore in 1814, after torching Washington, D.C. Their plan was to attack by land and sea, but thanks to the men and cannons of Fort McHenry and North Point, the British offensive failed.

The night of the attack, Francis Scott Key, a lawyer and private citizen, was waiting on an American sloop a few miles from shore. He was there to rescue his friend, Dr. Beanes, who was held hostage by the British. With the aid of the president, Key had secured a prisoner exchange that would take place after the battle for Fort McHenry was over.

What Francis Scott Key wrote that night, while waiting to rescue his friend, became "The Star Spangled Banner." And so the poem of a minor poet became the song of a new nation.

Baltimore was the second largest harbor in North America by 1850, but its glory days were fading by the 1950's. Gone were the bustling ship-building centers that served our nation in The Civil War, World War I and World War II.

According to the *Baltimore Harbor Manual*, Baltimore was perceived as "a city with a great past and no future." The young were leaving, and the Inner Harbor was decimated. Abandoned cars lined the streets and much of the harbor had become a place filled with toothless winos and rats.

Rescue missions aren't just for people; sometimes they are for cities as well, and it was clearly time for another mission. But this time Baltimore needed to save itself.

And it did. In 1954, Baltimore implemented the first plan in the United States that called for redevelopment of a downtown core: Baltimore's Charles Center. This was the first major effort to tackle the U.S.'s exodus to the suburbs. The future of Baltimore now rested on how well the people responded to the challenge of something called urban renewal. Once a city that chased after factories and smokestacks, it was now becoming a city that chased after people. By the 1970's, the entire city was changing, and along with it—the Inner Harbor, the heart of Baltimore.

Today, Baltimore is the flagship of the country; its urban renewal programs are studied and copied nationwide, while the city's downtown is currently undergoing *Baltimore's Second Renaissance*. Rumors are even starting that Baltimore will be the next hot spot for emerging high-tech and internet companies.

Because of the city's reincarnation, Baltimore has been called, "Charm City" or "America in Miniature," but the folks of Baltimore say it differently—"Welcome to Bawlamer, 'hon."

Pier 6 Concert Pavilion

Situated right on Baltimore's world-renowned Inner Harbor, Cavalier Telephone Pavilion at Pier Six is regarded by many as one of the most beautiful outdoor concert venues. The pavilion features famous-name entertainment during the spring and summer months.

Water Taxi

Park your car, because you won't need it to sightsee around the Inner Harbor. Instead, just hop aboard Baltimore's famous water taxis, seen here motoring across the harbor, and enjoy the journey as much as the destination. One fare is good all day, so you can enjoy spectacular waterfront views while you take these relaxing short-cuts across the harbor from one great attraction to the next.

7-Foot Knoll Lighthouse, Baltimore Maritime Museum

This odd-looking building is the oldest surviving screw-pile lighthouse. It was built in 1856 at the mouth of the Patapsco River, where it marked the shoal known as Seven-Foot Knoll for 133 years. Innovative technology suspended the lighthouse above the water by screwing its base into the soft mud of the sea floor, thus preventing the need for a typical underwater masonry foundation. In 1989 the Coast Guard donated it to the city to be preserved as a national landmark.

"Male/Female" Sculpture, Penn Station

When Jonathan Bororsky was a little boy, he would sit on his father's knee and talk to an imaginary, kind-hearted giant in the sky. Bororsky grew up to become an internationally acclaimed sculptor whose monumental works fill public plazas around the world. His 52' sculpture, in front of Penn Station, merges man with woman. Bororsky's sculptures would make his childhood friend very proud.

The Shot Tower (opposite)

This was once the tallest building in America, until the Washington Monument was built. This odd castle-keep of exactly one million bricks once was a foundry for ammunition. During the period from 1828 to 1892, molten lead was dropped from the top of the tower. On the way down, these lead "raindrops" formed into perfect spheres, cooling and solidifying as they fell into the water vat below.

Sea Monster Paddle Boats *(left)*

Hop aboard these colorful paddleboats and enjoy the Inner Harbor from the back of a sea monster. You can paddle over for a close-up view of the historic lightship Chesapeake and the submarine Torsk.

Lightship Chesapeake *(below)*

Built in 1930 as a floating lighthouse, the Lightship Chesapeake marked the entrance to the Chesapeake and Delaware Bays for almost 50 years. She was drafted into service during the Second World War, fitted with two rapid firing 20mm guns, and served as harbor patrol until peace returned.

USS Constellation *(opposite)*

The last Civil War vessel afloat, the U.S.S Constellation was built in 1854 and is the last all-sail warship built by the US Navy. After years of restoration, she was returned to the Inner Harbor on July 2, 1999.

Jones Falls Canal (above)

This promenade is typical of the kind of fresh personality that has become Baltimore; here birch trees begin their soothing rustle in early spring.

World Trade Center (opposite)

Located on the Inner Harbor, the Baltimore World Trade Center is the world's tallest equilateral five-sided building. It was designed by renowned architect I. M. Pei. The Trade Center houses the Maryland Port Administration, several state agencies, and numerous companies.

The Inner Harbor

Baltimore's Inner Harbor is one of America's oldest seaports, dating back to the 1600's. Chiefly an industrial port until the 1970's, it is the site of America's first successful downtown urban renewal project. Today this historic port's biggest industry is tourism, with 13 million visitors annually, making Baltimore the number one tourist destination in Maryland.

McCormick & Schmick's Seafood Restaurant, Pier 5, Inner Harbor

This waterside eatery, with stunning views of the harbor, is a long-time favorite with locals and a popular destination for tourists. Mouthwatering dishes such as Seafood Newburg and crab cakes keep diners coming back for more.

Baltimore Skyline at Night (above)

Nighttime is witness to the substance, sizzle, and sparkle of Baltimore's history-making reclamation and rebirth. Revitalized with hundreds of shops, seafood restaurants, museums, and tourist attractions, this Chesapeake Bay city is the number-one tourist destination in Maryland.

Marriott Waterfront Hotel (opposite)

Set on the edge of the Inner Harbor, the Marriott Waterfront is a short walk from the city's best dining, entertainment, and cultural venues, including Baltimore National Aquarium, Power Plant Live, ESPN Zone, Hard Rock Cafe, McCormick & Schmick's Restaurant, and the Cheesecake Factory.

World Trade Center and USS Constellation

The 19th century *U.S.S. Constellation* was the largest 'sloop' ever commissioned by the U.S. Navy and was able to outgun many of her adversaries. Because of her hidden firepower and advanced speed, she was nicknamed The Yankee Race Horse.

Marriott Waterfront Hotel

The Baltimore Marriott Waterfront Hotel dominates a prime piece of real estate along the Inner Harbor East shore. Rising thirty-two floors, the hotel delivers fabulous views of the city and the harbor.

Francis Scott Key Memorial Bridge

Opened in 1977, the bridge was named for Francis Scott Key (1780-1843), who wrote "The Star Spangled Banner" following the British attack on Baltimore in 1814. The final link in the 52-mile Baltimore Beltway, the bridge spans 1.6 miles across Baltimore Harbor and connects Sollers Point in Baltimore County with Hawkins Point in Baltimore City.

Marine Terminal (top)

"Keep the cargo moving" is the simple principle behind Baltimore Harbor's innovative and computerized marine terminals. This deep-water industrial port handles bulk cargoes such as grain, ore, and coal and also emerged in the 1990's as one of the nation's leading ports for automobile importing and exporting.

Commercial Ships at Northwest Harbor (bottom)

The Port of Baltimore serves America's Midwestern markets, as well as other ports along the Atlantic Coast. The Port has experienced an overall growth in commodity movements over the past 10 years. In 1999, more than 27,000 vessel calls and 37.3 million tons of cargo were handled in the Port.

The Old Power Plant

Turbines are gone, as are the boilers, the coal bins, and the power converters. Only the four smokestacks, threatened with removal for a time, have remained rough and ready reminders that the harbor was once about hard work, the kind that helped build a great nation.

Rusty Scupper Restaurant and Domino Sugar Factory

The neon Domino Sugar sign looms over the East River like a beacon, visible for miles. America's first sugar refinery, it once manufactured sixty percent of the nation's sugar, but now serves as a packaging and shipping center. Just next door, Rusty Scupper, a favorite seafood eatery, sits in the shadow of historic Federal Hill.

Renaissance Harborplace Hotel

This luxurious 12-story hotel showcases stunning waterfront views from the guest rooms and its fine dining restaurants. The hotel lobby is connected to *The Gallery*, a collection of more than 60 specialty shops and restaurants. The full-service Renaissance is the perfect destination for both business and leisure travelers, and is within walking distance of many downtown attractions.

Santa's Workshop, Harborplace *(above)*

Located center stage on the Inner Harbor, Harborplace is a feast for the senses all year round. During the Christmas holidays, it becomes a winter wonderland with seasonal fun and festivities, Santa's Place, Christmas carolers, and wonderful shops overflowing with great gift ideas.

The Inner Harbor at Night *(following page)*

Baltimore's unparalleled success redeveloping its decaying downtown core into a one billion dollar tourism boom for Maryland has been the model other struggling cities have turned to for inspiration in their own renewals.

Remnants of the Past at Canton Cove Park *(top)*

Rising out of the water against a backdrop of leisure boats is a rusty reminder from Canton Cove's earlier days as an industrial port that serviced smokestack industries such as a cotton mill, distillery, iron works and ship building.

Seaport Taxi *(bottom)*

Take water taxis between destinations on a personal historic tour around this famous harbor. Because Baltimore's seaport has been around for over 300 years, the historic areas range from Canton on the east through Fells Point, the Inner Harbor and Federal Hill, all the way to Fort McHenry in the south.

Jones Falls Canal

Jones Fall Canal cuts through Baltimore and creates lovely waterfront walks and views.

Rowhouses in Mount Vernon Neighborhood (left)

Mount Vernon encompasses the best of what city living has to offer. This area, so lively and stunning, is not only the cultural center of Baltimore, but a national treasure of 19th century style and architecture.

Rowhouses in Canton Neighborhood (below)

The Statue of Liberty greets passersby from the window of a formstone-covered row house in the historic Canton community. Canton was originally the waterfront plantation of Captain John O'Donnell, who sailed to Maryland from Canton, China at the close of the 19th century with a rich cargo of teas, china, silks and satins.

Graham-Hughes House (opposite)

This impressive home was designed as a French chateau by owner George Brown Graham and his family. There were circular window heads, a corbelled chimney, and a three-story turret topped with a turquoise finial. The amazing craftsmanship throughout this historic house shows just how many gifted artisans there were during this time in Baltimore.

Edgar Allen Poe House and Grave *(opposite and above)*

Although Richmond, Virginia is the place Poe most considered home, Baltimore defines the beginning and the end of his life. He was born in Boston in 1809 while his parents, both actors, were away from their Baltimore home. Nearly 200 years later, Poe remains one of the America's greatest writers and is known as the Father of the Detective Story, the Short Story, and the Horror Story. He is also remembered for his frightening poem, 'The Raven.' Poe lived in the house, shown here, with his wife in 1843. Today, he rests with his wife and aunt under the monument erected for him in Baltimore's Westminster Graveyard.

Rowhouses in Canton Neighborhood (above)

The row houses that line the streets of Baltimore's historic Canton neighborhood are a product of over one hundred years of planned development begun in the 1820's by the *Canton Company*, a real estate developer who owned three thousand acres in the area.

Historic Rolando-Thom House, Bolton Hill (opposite)

This historic house in the Bolton Hill neighborhood now houses *Family and Children's Services of Central Maryland*, a social services agency founded in 1849. People are invited to stroll through the adjacent Memorial Garden that celebrates and honors the human spirit.

Rowhouses on Bolton Street, Bolton Hill

The historic neighborhood of Bolton Hill sits on slopes within walking distance of Baltimore's cultural center. In the 1920's and 30's, artists and writers such as F. Scott Fitzgerald gave the area a reputation as the city's Jazz Age Bohemian district. Today, restored 19th-century mansion homes and modern town homes with marble front stoops complement the tranquil, tree lined streets and quaint urban parks.

Formstone Façade Rowhouses in Canton Neighborhood

A stroll down the historic streets of Canton is a lesson in architecture and history. In the mid 20th century, many brick row houses were covered in formstone (below), a low-cost material that insulated and covered up deteriorating brickwork. Formstone continues to cover many façades today. The artistic tradition of screen paintings also abounds in Canton, originally started by a grocer in 1913 when he adorned the window screens of his shop with paintings of meats and vegetables.

Little Italy (top and bottom)

Little Italy is a vibrant neighborhood in the heart of the downtown renaissance in Baltimore. Located between the Inner Harbor and Historic Fells Point, the area boasts more than twenty of Maryland's best Italian restaurants and trattorias.

Howard Street (opposite)

Any walking tour of downtown Baltimore should include Howard Street's "Antique Row" where over 75 dealers showcase items from as far back as the 1700's to the 20th century's Art Deco period.

The Wharf Rat Brew Pub, Fells Point

The stately oil portrait, the shaving cup collection, the model ships, and the golden Buddha are just a few of the eclectic touches you'll find at this Fells Point pub. While it's true they brew the beer on Pratt Street, it's the ambiance of the Wharf Rat that charms 'em all.

Lexington Market, Lexington Street (top)

Opened in 1782, Lexington Market is the world's largest continuously running market. As old as the nation itself, this wonderful Baltimore tradition is still located at the original site where it opened for business over 220 years ago.

Café on Pratt Street (bottom)

Pratt Street is the location of the oldest Irish pub in America, Patrick's. Restored to original condition in many of its details, the pub was opened in 1847, the same year Thomas Edison and Alexander Graham Bell were born.

Fells Point Waterfront

One of America's oldest surviving maritime communities, Fells Point's cobblestone streets brim over with charming shops, galleries, pubs, and restaurants. This national historic district proudly boasts of 350 original residential structures, many dating to the early 1700's.

A. T. Jones & Sons on Howard Street (top)

Whether you are an opera star in need of a costume for "La Boheme" or just want to be the star of your Halloween party, this is your place. The shop's owner is a professional costume designer and the director of the Baltimore Opera House.

Park Avenue Pharmacy Window, Bolton Hill (bottom)

Even the local pharmacy reflects the artistic bohemian traditions of this historic neighborhood, an area made famous in the 1920's and '30s when it attracted artists, musicians and writers of the flamboyant Jazz Age. F. Scott Fitzgerald wrote his classic "Tender is the Night" while living here.

Fells Point Waterfront (above)

With its cobblestone streets and waterfront location, historic Fells Point has long been a favorite attraction for locals and tourists who come to enjoy its eclectic collection of stores, boutiques, and restaurants.

Claddagh Pub, O'Donnell Square, Canton (opposite)

A popular neighborhood pub, its name, Claddagh, celebrates a 400-year-old Irish tradition. A master goldsmith in an Irish fishing village created the original design for a ring, or "claddagh" which symbolizes the virtues of love, friendship, and loyalty—a crown above a heart held by two hands.

The Recreation Pier, Fells Point (left)

Recreation Pier was built in 1916 by the city as a safe play space for neighborhood children. In the mid-1990s, the abandoned pier served as the location for the television series, Homicide. Today, Fells Point entertains visitors with its popular Ghost Tour, an evening walk around the neighborhood while the tour guide tells tales of spirits, history, and lore.

The Speakeasy Salon, O'Donnell Street (below)

Come inside the Speakeasy Saloon and step back in time to the free-spirited Roaring Twenties. There are rumors that the perfect martini resides within these walls—not to mention wonderful and daring pasta, meat, and seafood dishes. Don't forget to tell them that Joe sent you!

The Stafford Hotel (opposite)

Built in 1898 by Charles Cassell, the elegant Stafford Hotel was the preferred residence of visiting celebrities and the cream of society. The hotel closed in 1972 and re-opened as the Stafford Apartments.

Zion Church of the City of Baltimore From City Hall Dome (above)

When German Lutherans began settling in Baltimore Town in the 1730's, they worshipped in their homes. As their numbers grew, so did the need for a church. Built originally in 1755, Zion Church was rebuilt twice, evolving over the centuries into an important center for the social and spiritual life of Lutherans in Baltimore.

City Hall (opposite)

When the rapid growth of Baltimore in the mid-19th century proved too much for the original city hall to handle, the taxpayers voted to build the present City Hall. Designed by architect George A. Frederick and built in 1875, the building is a rare example of the French Second Empire style being used in an American government building. This distinctive structure was, surprisingly, the first commission of 22-year-old architect, George Frederick and cost $200,000 dollars to build.

City Hall Interiors (left and below)

In 1977, the city of Baltimore voted to renovate the old City Hall rather than build a new one. As part of extensive renovations that doubled City Hall's office space, the exquisite, stained glass dome was painstakingly disassembled and put back together (bottom photo). Today the marble rotunda, with its elaborate, inlaid wood floor design, is open to an admiring public.

City Hall (opposite)

Renovations of City Hall include a magnificent restoration of the Ceremonial Chambers, an ornate space reminiscent of Buckingham Palace. The mayor of Baltimore receives important guests, honors special individuals, and make important public announcements here.

Downtown Building Details (top and bottom)

Downtown Baltimore is the address of one of the most ambitious and successful revitalizations in America today. Over one billion dollars was recently earmarked from city, state, and private institutions for what many are calling 'Baltimore's Second Renaissance.'

Bromo Seltzer Tower (opposite)

A Baltimore landmark since its construction in 1911, the Emerson Bromo-Seltzer Tower was built by Capt. Isaac Emerson, the inventor of the headache remedy Bromo-Seltzer. It was designed by Joseph Evans Sperry (also designer of the Baltimore Brewers Exchange). At that time, it was the tallest building in the city.

Pratt Street Architecture *(above and opposite)*

Downtown Baltimore is a working model for how a city can be progressive while still protecting its unique heritage. Two downtown historic districts include many turn-of-the-century, brick buildings representative of Romanesque, Victorian, and early modern industrial architecture styles. Several are still commercial; however, others are chic, residential loft spaces.

The Engineers Club, Garret-Jacobs Mansion

Most of the original Mt. Vernon buildings remain today, but their functions have changed. The Garret-Jacobs Mansion is now the Engineers Club.

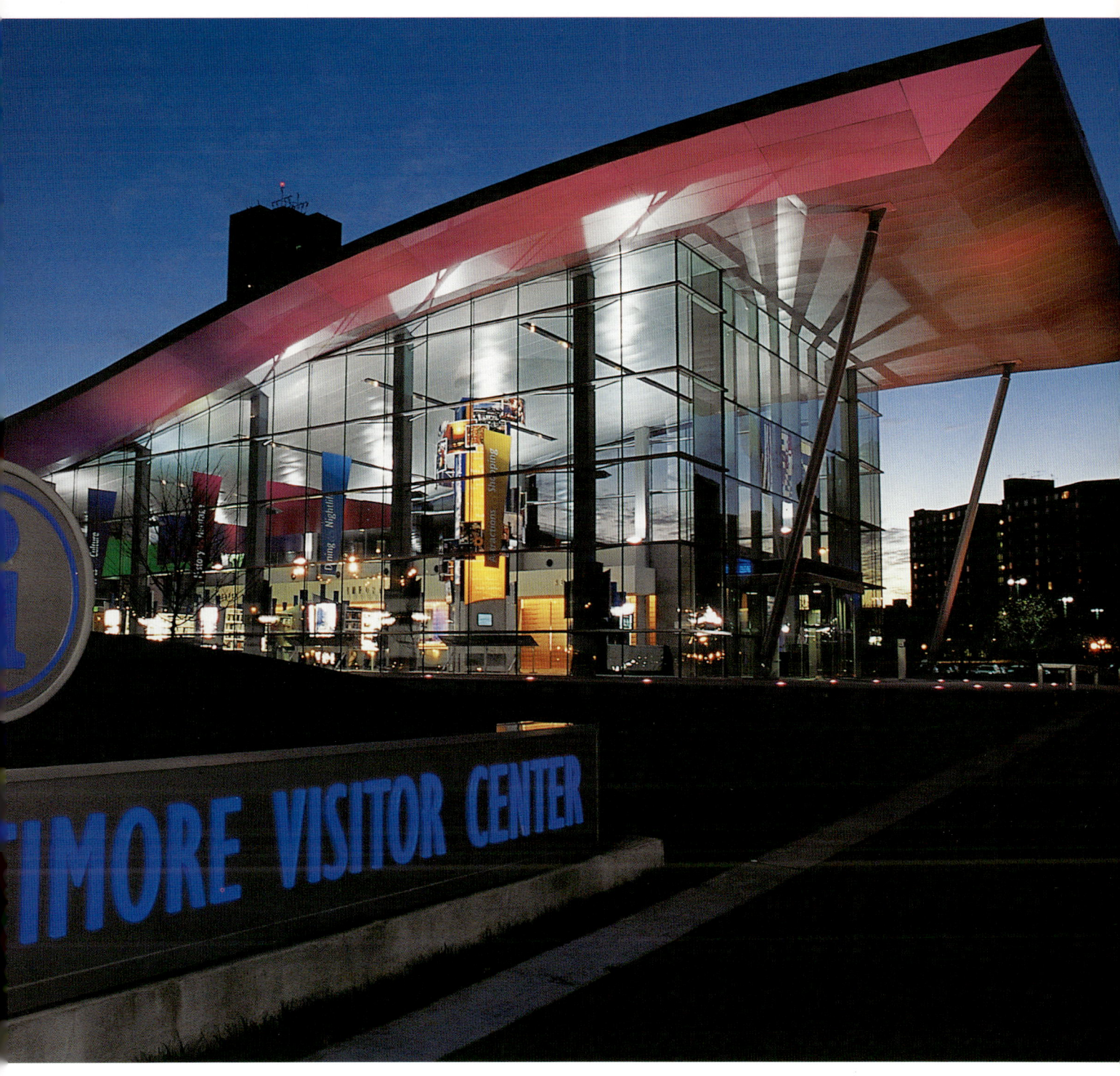

Baltimore Visitors Center, Inner Harbor

As a starting point for planning your stay in Baltimore, the new Visitors Center is the perfect way to get information about the city's history, attractions, events, accommodations, entertainment, and dining.

Baltimore Skyline from Carroll Park (above)

Carroll Park in southwest Baltimore contributed greatly to the early development of the city park system. In addition to a panoramic view of the downtown skyline, the 117-acre park has a golf course, outdoor skating rink, and playground.

Hippodrome Theater, France-Merrick Performing Arts Center (opposite)

Baltimore's historic vaudeville theater was built in 1914 and later became one of the first theaters in the city to show motion pictures. After being closed for 14 years, it was renovated and made part of the performing arts center in 2004.

Zion Church of the City of Baltimore *(above)*

The understated architecture of Zion Church is the perfect framing for the exquisite stained and leaded glass windows throughout the sanctuary. In this panel, three female figures symbolize "Faith, Hope and Love," one of five windows that depict the life of Christ.

Zion Church of the City of Baltimore *(opposite)*

The bell tower of Zion Church once inspired a well-known writer to exclaim, "This Is the German cathedral of Baltimore." With its arcades and low-walled garden, Zion Church is part of today's beautiful Baltimore Civic Center area.

Grace and St. Peter's Church *(above)*

This Gothic church was opened in 1852 and was the first brownstone building in Baltimore. A stone copy of Leonardo da Vinci's *Last Supper* adorns the altar's back wall. Nineteenth-century style stain glass windows are located throughout the church.

Lovely Lane United Methodist Church *(opposite)*

This magnificent, national historic landmark church was designed by famed architect Stanford White and built in 1884. Its history is celebrated in the church museum with exhibits, portraits, and memorabilia from its founders.

The Prince Hall Grand Lodge of Maryland (above)

Even though this building is now the site of a Masonic Grand Lodge, the round windows with six-point stars reveal the Jewish legacy of its previous occupant, Temple of Oheb Shalom, a synagogue whose congregation dates back to 1853.

St. Michael the Archangel Ukranian Catholic Church, Eastern Avenue (opposite)

Western Ukrainians began immigrating to the Fells Point area of Baltimore in the 1880's. The present church, completed in 1991, showcases the distinctive golden domes of Byzantine churches that symbolize heaven.

The First Franklin St. Presbyterian Church *(opposite)*

One of the oldest churches in Baltimore, this is a spectacular example of Gothic Revival architecture and is recognized on the National Register of Historic Places. It will be celebrating its 250th anniversary in 2011.

Walters Art Museum *(above)*

The museum is internationally recognized for its collections of world art from pre-dynastic Egypt to 20th-century Europe. Its treasures include Greek sculpture, Roman sarcophagi, medieval ivories, Old Master paintings, Art Deco jewelry and 19th-century masterpieces.

Maryland Institute College of Art, Bolton Hill

Founded in 1826, MICA is the oldest accredited art college in America and consistently ranks among the nation's top programs in visual arts and design.

Maryland Institute College of Art

Boldly sculpted lines define the award-winning Brown Center for digital arts and design. The center is the first new academic building constructed on this eclectic, urban campus in nearly a century.

The Cloisters, Brooklandville *(above and opposite)*

The Cloisters is a magnificent 1932 mansion on 60 acres in nearby Brooklandville. The original owners, Mr. & Mrs. Parker, designed it themselves, basing the house on late medieval French and English architecture they had admired during their European travels. The interior beams of oak, chestnut, and walnut were hand hewn by craftsmen on site. Most of the ironwork, including the railing for the spectacular spiral stair tower, was designed by Mr. Parker and produced in his ironworks. The Parkers bequeathed the estate to Baltimore, and it is now a popular setting for weddings and other social functions.

71

Bromo Seltzer Tower Clock *(left and below)*

This historic landmark structure was modeled after the Palazzo Vecchio in Florence, Italy and completed in 1911. The illuminated tower was originally topped with a 51-foot revolving replica of the blue Bromo-Seltzer bottle, which could be seen from 20 miles away. The four clock faces are all still working; however, the bottle had to be removed in 1936 due to structural problems. The public missed the blue glow so much that modern lighting techniques have recreated 'the bromo blue' at the tower's top.

Bromo Seltzer Towers Mural *(opposite)*

The tower's dramatic mural is the result of the efforts of the Baltimore Mural Program, which actively engages artists and local residents in "art beautification" projects involving mural art.

Christopher Columbus Statue, Inner Harbor (above)

Carved in vivid white Italian Carrara marble, this remarkable monument pays tribute to Christopher Columbus. The figure faces east toward Europe and captures the power and boldness of the world explorer who discovered America.

National Katyn Memorial (opposite)

In 1943, the mass graves of 20,000 Polish officers were discovered in the Katyn Forest by Nazi troops. The officers had been rounded up by Russian forces and murdered. This startlingly dramatic monument mourns those victims and their families and celebrates great Polish war heros and leaders.

Statue of Orpheus, Fort McHenry *(left)*

At the fort's entrance, visitors are greeted by a large bronze statue of the Greek hero, Orpheus, atop a marble pedestal. The monument, by sculptor Charles Niehaus, is dedicated to Francis Scott Key and the soldiers and sailors who fought the Battle of North Point and defended Fort McHenry during the War of 1812.

Captain John O'Donnell, Canton Neighborhood *(below)*

O'Donnell was the first trader to sail into Baltimore Harbor with a valuable cargo of goods from Canton, China in the late 19th century. By the mid-1800's, the plantation was a hub of commercial and industrial development, heavily influenced by the new B&O Railroad. His original waterfront plantation is the site of Baltimore's historic Canton neighborhood. O'Donnell and his descendants were enormously important catalysts in the development of Baltimore as a major port city.

Lafayette Statue, South Washington Place *(opposite)*

This striking, equestrian statue depicts Revolutionary War hero General Lafayette. The statue is dedicated to the memory of the fallen American and French comrades of World War I.

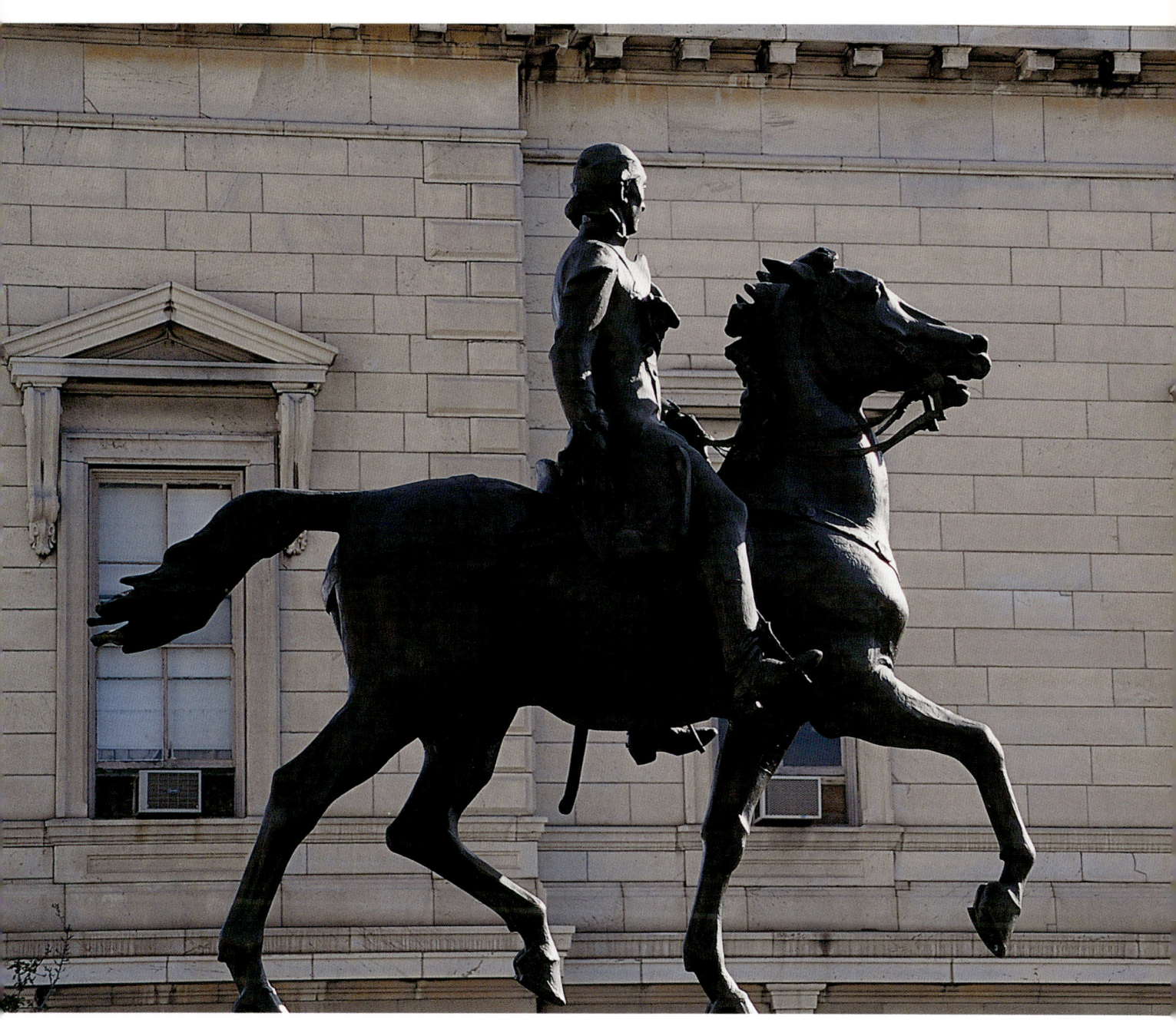

Newly Restored Sculpture by Linda DePalma *(opposite)*

This popular outdoor sculpture by local sculptor and educator Linda DePalma was recently restored to the delight of Baltimoreans.

Pulaski Monument, Patterson Park *(above)*

General Kazimierz Pulaski was one of several Polish heroes of the American Revolution. Pulaski organized a cavalry brigade and became known as the Father of the American Cavalry.

Children Folding Flag, Fort McHenry

Fort McHenry's bombardment and Francis Scott Key's writing of "The Star-Spangled Banner" are commemorated each September with festivities that include the ceremonial procession of a replica flag, battle reenactments, and concerts culminating in fireworks.

National Monument and Historic Shrine, Fort McHenry *(right)*

During the War of 1812, one thousand Americans under the leadership of Major General Armistead at Fort McHenry successfully defended the Baltimore harbor and stopped a British advance into the city.

Armistead Statue, Fort McHenry *(below)*

Major George Armistead was the commander of Fort McHenry's successful defense during the 1814 bombardment by British forces. Months before the battle, Armistead ordered a flag to be made for Ft. McHenry that would be so large that the British would have no trouble seeing it from a distance. Miles from shore, lawyer and amateur poet Francis Scott Key saw the flag and was so inspired that he wrote the poem that became America's national anthem.

Star Spangled Banner Centennial Monument (*above*)

During the War of 1812, American troops stood ready during the decisive battle of North Point at "Hampstead Hill," Patterson Park's promontory where the Pagoda is now situated. The newly restored 1891 pagoda reflects Baltimoreans' fascination with the Orient.

Fells Point Maritime Museum (*opposite*)

From the 1730's until the mid-19th century, Fells Point was the center of Baltimore's maritime commerce. Shipbuilders, immigrants, merchants, and sailors sought their fortunes in this waterfront community, home to the world-famous Baltimore clipper schooners.

Francis Scott Key Monument (*above and opposite*)

It was the valiant defense of Fort McHenry by American forces during the British attack on September 13, 1814 that inspired 35-year-old poet-lawyer Francis Scott Key to write the poem that became our national anthem. The poem was written to match the meter of the English song, "To Anacreon In Heaven." "The Star-Spangled Banner" became our official national anthem in 1931.

American Visionary Museum (top and bottom)

This unique museum only exhibits the works of self-taught artists, the message being that America is at her best when she actively remembers that many of her greatest citizens were self-taught, self-made pioneers.

Gloria Victis Statue (opposite)

This statue is a memorial to Frederick Douglass, the famed abolitionist who lived here in the 1820's and '30s, prior to his escape from slavery.

Korean War Memorial, Canton Water Park *(opposite)*

This memorial pays tribute to the 527 Maryland citizens who died in hostile action during the Korean War, as well as those still listed as missing in action in that conflict.

Lafayette Statue, Mount Vernon Place *(above)*

This statue honors General Lafayette, the first private French citizen to help the American colonies fight the War of Independence from England. The Gothic spires of Mount Vernon Place United Methodist Church rise majestically in the background.

West Mount Vernon Place Architectural Detail
(above and opposite)

Once homes to rail barons, diplomats, bankers, philanthropists and socialites, the magnificent buildings of the Mt. Vernon Place neighborhood are an unparalleled collection of historic 19th century architecture along wide boulevards. In the background, the dark Gothic spire of historic Mount Vernon Place United Methodist Church soars high over this elegant, old-world community.

Trains Bringing Cargo To and From the Port of Baltimore (*above*)

Trains have been a constant workhorse in the Port of Baltimore, picking up, delivering, and transporting containers of everything from grains to automobiles.

National Aquarium (*opposite*)

The National Aquarium.is one of the last jewels set in the Inner Harbor's sparkling crown of attractions. Watch sharks up close, walk in a tropical rain forest, or visit the 10,000 sea creatures that swim, scuttle, and cling to our world.

Civil War Museum, Inner Harbor East *(above)*

Housed in one of the oldest train stations in the nation, the museum examines the violent events of April 19, 1861, the infamous day when Baltimore became the place where the first Civil War blood was shed. Exhibits highlight Maryland's divided loyalties and critical role as a border state during the war.

George Peabody Library, Johns Hopkins University *(opposite)*

This 1878 sanctuary of learning has a 300,000-volume collection of books that includes Greek and Latin classics, and British and American history and literature, to name a few categories. Architecturally stunning, this library features a black-and-white marble floor and a six-story skylight atrium surrounded by cast iron balconies.

Cyburn Arboretum *(above and opposite)*

Cyburn Arboretum is a 207-acre nature preserve and city park on the grounds of a luxurious post-Civil War mansion. The mansion is the location of Baltimore City's horticultural headquarters and home of the Cylburn Arboretum Association.

Maryland Zoo (above)

After a $1.3 million renovation, the former Baltimore Zoo reopened in spring 2005 with a new name and a new look and is drawing larger crowds than ever.

Maryland Science Center (opposite)

Two hundred years after it first opened its doors as an amateur scientific society in 1797, The Maryland Science Center celebrated a grand re-opening showing off its new atrium, IMAX theater, stunning observatory, expanded Kids' Room, and an amazing Dinosaur Hall.

Museum of Industry (above and opposite)

From food canning to broadcasting, museum visitors can experience the technologies of the Industrial Revolution that catapulted Baltimore into the 21st century. Step into vividly-recreated workshops and the only surviving cannery building. Experience local innovations firsthand which touched the world, from the first disposable bottle cap to America's first umbrella company. There is plenty more to see outside, too—a World War II flying boat bomber, a unique steam tugboat, and coal-fired S.S. Baltimore.

Baltimore Public Works Museum, Inner Harbor
(above, left and opposite)

The historic Eastern Avenue Pumping Station is a fitting home for the Baltimore Public Works Museum where visitors explore the fascinating technology behind clean water, wastewater, recycling, tunnels, roads, and bridges. Exhibits showcase Baltimore's earliest public works projects and illustrate how today's Public Works services shape our city and environment. Kids will love exploring "Streetscape," an outdoor maze of drains, conduits, and pipes.

Baltimore Museum of Art *(left, below and opposite)*

In the early 20th century, two Baltimore sisters, Claribel and Etta Cone, assembled one of the most important private art collections in the world, which was subsequently bequeathed to the museum. The sisters visited the Paris studios of Henri Matisse and Pablo Picasso and acquired exceptional pieces. They also collected paintings by Cézanne, Gauguin, van Gogh, Renoir, and international textile art. Today the Cone Collection is one of several permanent collections housed in this stately 1929 Neo-classical building. Other collections showcase Contemporary Art, American Paintings and Decorative Arts, European Paintings and Sculpture, Arts of Africa, Asia, The Americas and Oceania, and a Sculpture Garden.

Homewood House Museum, Johns Hopkins University *(top)*

Homewood House Museum is on the university campus and is one of the finest surviving examples of Federal Period architecture. After several years of research and restoration, it was reopened to the public in 1987.

The Johns Hopkins University *(above and opposite)*

Founded in 1876, Johns Hopkins University was the first research university in the United States. This new educational enterprise emphasized the importance of research and its enhancement of the educational process, changing the course of American education.

Baltimore Conservatory & Botanic Garden, Druid Hill Park *(above and opposite)*

The Baltimore Conservatory resides in a sparkling glass greenhouse that dates back to the 1880s and showcases a wonderful collection of international flora. The domed Palm House, in the original room of this historic conservatory, is shown on the right.

Baltimore Conservatory & Botanic Garden, Druid Hill Park *(above and opposite)*

After major renovations, the Conservatory reopened in 2004 with climate controlled greenhouses that mimic the diverse global climates of the desert, the tropics, and the Mediterranean. Visitors also enjoy the exotic and legendary flowers in the Conservatory's Orchid Room.

Outside, a prolific garden of 35 flower beds surrounds the conservatory with a profuse rainbow of blooms and blossoms from early Spring until late Fall.

Maryland Historical Society, Druid Hill Park (top)

One of America's oldest and largest state historical centers, the Society was founded in 1844 and oversees one of the largest collections of Americana in the world and publishes books about Maryland's rich history.

Antique Row (bottom)

Antique lovers know all about the treasures to be found on Howard Street. Over 75 antique dealers in a concentrated area give shoppers a tremendous inventory of nostalgic wares dating as far back as the 1700's up to the newer classics of the 20th century.

Maryland Renaissance Festival, Crownsville, MD

The Renaissance Festival has entertained people for nearly 30 years, offering a peek at life in Europe 600 years ago. The walled village of Revel Grove is a replica of a 16th-century English village and is set on a beautiful 125-acre wooded site which includes a Jousting Arena, eight cottages, five pubs, and plenty of free parking.

Maryland Renaissance Festival

This popular historical festival in the walled village of Revel Grove has grown up to be the region's premier outdoor event and the second largest Renaissance Festival in America. More than 1,300 men, women, and children participate in this large theme show and approximately 225,000 people attend annually.

Columbus Day Parade

When Columbus Day arrives, Baltimore throws a citywide party and everyone is invited. The celebration is the nation's oldest and longest continuous Columbus Day celebration.

Wall Mural, Across from B&O Railroad Museum

Though not officially associated with the Museum, this mural of an old 'cattle-catcher' locomotive does, like the museum, appear to be caught in time.

The B&O Railroad Museum

Trains were once the lifeblood of America's growth, and here, at the Mt. Claire Station, is where it all began. The B&O Railroad Museum, an affiliate of the Smithsonian Institution, celebrates this special chapter in American history. It opened slightly more than a century after the B&O Railroad completed the nation's first railroad line from the Atlantic tidewater to the Ohio River.

The B&O Railroad Museum (above and opposite)

The 40-acre historic site, regarded as the "Birthplace of American Railroading" is home to the oldest, most comprehensive collection of railroad artifacts in the Western Hemisphere, including an unparalleled roster of 150 nineteenth and twentieth-century locomotives and rolling stock. The museum includes the 1851 Mt. Clare Station, America's first railroad station, the 1884 Baldwin Roundhouse, and the first mile of commercial railroad track in America. Visitors enjoy train rides and a 60-ft "HO" train layout inside of a vintage passenger coach.

The Babe Ruth Birthplace *(above)*

Babe Ruth did not have a happy childhood. By the age of seven, he was sent to a reformatory and orphanage and rarely saw his parents for twelve years. Unruly and labeled as incorrigible, he found a father figure in one of the school's teachers, Brother Matthias, who became an inspiration to him in baseball and other aspects of life.

Babe Ruth Birthplace & Statue *(above and opposite)*

When attendance at baseball games was declining due to the 1919 Black Sox scandal, Babe Ruth's bat saved the day. He began his professional career with the Baltimore Orioles and in no time, the Babe turned baseball on its head, exciting disillusioned fans and single-handedly re-energizing the sport.

Ravens Walk *(above)*

The M & T Stadium is the new home of the Baltimore Ravens, Baltimore's NFL franchise. The stadium, located in downtown Baltimore, is immediately adjacent to Oriole Park at Camden Yards, home of the Baltimore Orioles.

Johnny Unitas Statue, M&T Bank Stadium *(opposite)*

Johnny Unitas was a Baltimore Colt for seventeen years. The 'Golden Arm' was recently voted as a member of the "Quarterback of the Century Team." Of all the records he set, one still remains the grandest in NFL history: he delivered a touchdown pass in 47 consecutive games.

Oriole Park, Camden Yards *(above and opposite)*

Oriole fans found something else to love about baseball when Oriole Park at Camden Yards, a beautiful baseball-only park, became the official home of the Orioles in 1992. The park was built on the site of Camden Yards, an old railroad center. Interestingly, the Orioles' new home is only two blocks from the birthplace of baseball's legendary hero, "Babe" Ruth.

Oriole Park, Camden Yards (*above and opposite*)

Camden Yards has given a big boost to Baltimore's downtown area. The park is a 10-minute walk from Baltimore's Inner Harbor and is convenient to literally hundreds of restaurants, bars, and shops within walking distance of the ballpark. Baseball enthusiasts enjoy taking a guided tour of Oriole Park to experience the coveted, behind-the-scenes views from the club-level suites, press box, scoreboard control room, and dugouts.

Jake McGuire is known for his striking photos of American cities and landscapes. His photos appear in private collections, exhibitions, offices, and are often found in airline and travel magazines. He has won 11 awards for photography and photojournalism. In January of 1989, the Presidential Inaugural Committee commissioned McGuire to produce a signed, limited edition print of the White House. It was signed by the President and Vice President and given to those who performed at the Inaugural Gala. In March of 1992, McGuire received an Arts America grant from the United States Information Agency to give photography lectures in the Persian Gulf Sheikdom of Bahrain. In April of 1997, *LIFE MAGAZINE* selected one of McGuire's photos for the cover of a special edition of *LIFE*. In August of 2004, McGuire joined forces with Twin Lights Publishers to produce a series of colorful photographic journals. Titles that are currently available include, *Washington, D.C.: A Photographic Portrait, Baltimore, MD: A Photographic Portrait, and Annapolis, MD: A Photographic Portrait*. He is also working on a book on the coast of New England to be released in the summer of 2006. See more of Jake's work at www.jakemcguire.com.

Special thanks to Anna Katalkina for finding and contacting places in Baltimore to be included in this book.